MW01025368

Peace in the Storm

Bertha J. & Keith M. Seiber
2020bible.club

Acts 20:20 *"And how I kept back nothing that was profitable unto you, but have shewed you, and have taught you publickly, and from house to house,"*

20/20 Bible Club

Acts 20:20

Bible quotations are taken from The King
James Version of the Bible.

First Printing: 2016

ISBN 978-1-329-90850-5

20/20 Bible Club Publications
10633 Peaceful Drive
Demotte, IN 46310

www.2020bible.club

Like us on facebook -
facebook.com/2020bibleclub

Ordering Information: Please go to our website
2020bible.club and click on the Bookstore tab
or go to
www.lulu.com/spotlight/2020bibleclub.

Dedication

The genesis of this book is from some writings I found of my mothers. At the writing of this book she has just recently went to be with Jesus in Heaven. As I was going through some of her papers I found a notebook with some notes she had written about the Word of God and truths she had learned from His Word.

This find meant a lot to me and comforted me. The more I read her words and comments about truths she had learned, I realized how great and insightful they were. I wanted to share them with others. Most of parts two and three are my mother's writings and thoughts. I added some to each of these parts and added a few cross references; but the majority of both of these sections are her writings and her words. The other sections are my writings.

I am dedicating this book to her memory. To the memory and testimony of Bertha Jean Seiber – a great and extremely loving mother – from her son who forever will be indebted to how she raised me, what she has done for me, and the path she set me on for my life. I am grateful and honored to include her as a co-author of this book. – Thank you Mother!

With Love, you are greatly missed. - Keith

This picture of my mother was taken December 24th, 2015 just two days before she went to be with our Lord in Heaven.

Contents

Page 9 – *Part 1* – **"*If Need Be*"**

Page 23 – *Part 2* – **God is What we Need!**

Page 29 – *Part 3* – **Trusting God in the Trial**

Page 37 – *Part 4* – **Encourage Yourself in the Lord**

Page 53 – *Part 5* – **Inquire at the Lord for Direction**

Page 69 – *Part 6* – **"*God is our Refuge and Strength*"**

Page 83 – **References**

Peace in the Storm - Part 1

"If Need Be"

"If Need Be"

> *I Peter 1:6-7* – *"Wherein ye greatly rejoice, though now for a season, if need be, ye are in heaviness through manifold temptations: That the trial of your faith, being much more precious than of gold that perisheth, though it be tried with fire, might be found unto praise and honour and glory at the appearing of Jesus Christ."*

INTRODUCTION: When we go through a trial there can be many reasons this trial is happening. We need to look to God in the trial. Trust God in the trial. See how God can use us to help others in the trial. Perhaps we can be a comfort to others going through a similar trial that we have made it through. In a trial we tend to recognize our total dependence on God, but in reality, that is how we should view all parts of our life, whether we are currently going through a trial or not.

THE PARADOX OF THE TRIAL. "If need be" (*I Peter 1:6*). The word "Paradox" means an argument that produces an inconsistency, typically within logic or common sense. Well, to my finite thinking I could not think of a need to go through a trial. I would rather have everything go perfect all the time. This is where the paradox comes in because *I Peter 1:6* says *"if need be, ye are in heaviness through manifold temptations:"* "*Manifold temptations*" – means various trials you may be going through. The Lord may see a reason to put us through the trial but we may not see the reason at the time.

I have written down four reasons for trials, not the only reasons, but four for us to consider.

1. **Repentance** – *Acts 8:22* – *"Repent therefore of this thy wickedness, and pray God, if perhaps the thought of thine heart may be forgiven thee."*

2. **Reliance** – *Psalm 20:7-8* – *"Some trust in chariots, and some in horses: but we will remember the name of the LORD our God. They are brought down and fallen: but we are risen, and stand upright."*

3. **Refinement** – *II Corinthians 3:18* – *"But we all, with open face beholding as in a glass the glory of the Lord, are changed into the same image from glory to glory, even as by the Spirit of the Lord."*

4. **Revival** – *Psalm 80:19* – *"Turn us again, O LORD God of*

hosts, cause thy face to shine; and we shall be saved."

THE PRECIOUSNESS OF THE TRIAL. *"being much more precious than of gold"* (*I Peter 1:7*) When faced with a trial, our goal should be to, *"be found unto praise and honour and glory"*; like it says in verse 7. We need to guard our testimony in the trial. God will prepare us for bigger and better things through a trial. Remember David did not fight Goliath out of the blue one day. He first fought a lion, then a bear, and then he fought Goliath. Trials can be precious, because if we let Him, God can use them to make us more like Christ.

Know the Lord is close to you in the trial. One of my favorite poems to illustrate this is Footprints in the Sand. When the man asks God why? During the hardest times of my life is their just one set of footprints; and the Lord replies "it was then that I carried you!" This illustrates the preciousness of the closeness of the Lord during the trial.

Illustration – There was a preacher in the early 1900's that had a passion for souls. He was doing much for God. Many people were being saved everywhere he went to preach. He went through a trial "*If needs be*" like Peter said. The Lord used him in this trial to help someone at the time and the tale of this trial is still helping others today.

In 1912 he was crossing the Atlantic to come to Chicago to preach. His name was John Harper; some of you may know the story. On April 14, 1912 the unthinkable happened; the ship he was on struck an iceberg and began to sink, the ships name was the Titanic.

It was reported that Harper shouted "*Let the women, children and the unsaved in the lifeboats*". He gave his lifejacket to another man after asking him if he was saved and the man replied "*No*". He handed his 6 year old daughter to the deck captain with instructions she get put in a lifeboat.

The Titanic sank 2:45 minutes later. For fifty fearful minutes after that, there was piercing cries of people drowning in the dark frigid water. One thousand five hundred and twenty-two drown that night. Harper was one of them. During the final minutes a man drifting on a loose board came near Harper and Harper shouted to him "*Are you saved?*" the man replied "*NO*". Harper then quoted **Acts 16:31** to him "*Believe on the Lord Jesus Christ, and thou shalt be saved,*" The man drifted off still unsaved. A few minutes later he drifted back toward Harper who again shouted "*Are you saved?!!*" And he repeated **Acts 16:31** again "*Believe on the Lord Jesus Christ, and thou shalt be saved,*" to the man.

Those were the last words anyone heard the Preacher say as he slipped under the water for the last time. That man he witnessed to accepted Jesus Christ as his Savior. John Harper was loyal to God even in this trial unto death he was facing.

We need to learn to trust God with the trials and the Joys. Be found faithful to our Savior when you are being tested. Let your testimony be used unto the furtherance of the Gospel!

THE PRAISE IN THE TRIAL. (*I Peter 1:6-8* - *Wherein ye greatly rejoice, though now for a season, if need be, ye are in heaviness through manifold temptations: That the trial of your faith, being much more precious than of gold that perisheth, though it be tried with fire, might be found unto praise and honour and glory at the appearing of Jesus Christ: Whom having not seen, ye love; in whom, though now ye see him not, yet believing, ye rejoice with joy unspeakable and full of glory:)* We are to rejoice in trials, rejoice in heaviness. Though our faith "*be tried by fire*" we need to praise the one who died for us. We need to give praise to the Lord through our trial.

If you are going through a trial, it could be the Lord thinks you are ready to grow more in Him- it could be He thinks He can use you more for having gone through this trial. *I Peter 1:8* tells us *"Whom having not seen, ye love; in whom, though now ye see him not, yet believing, ye rejoice with joy unspeakable and full of glory:"* **Jeremiah 17:7** says *"Blessed is the man that trusteth in the LORD, and whose hope the LORD is."* Your attitude in a trial can make or break you. Verse 6 tells us to *"Greatly rejoice"* in the trial.

THE POSITION OF SECURITY IN THE TRIAL. *(I Peter 1:5 - Who are kept by the power of God through faith unto salvation ready to be revealed in the last time.)* We are kept by the power of God. He has all power. We can trust in His love and power to see us through the trial. But how are we kept by the power of God in a trial?

Verse 5 tells us it is *"through faith"*. Our faith in the all powerful God sees us through our trials. It takes faith to get us through the trial. **Hebrews 11:1** says *"Now faith is the substance of things hoped for, the evidence of things not seen. **Romans 8:31** says "What shall we then say to these things? If God be for us, who can be against us?"* And **Galatians 2:20** tells us "*I am crucified with Christ: nevertheless I live; yet not I, but Christ liveth in me: and the life which I now live in the flesh I live by the faith of the Son of God, who loved me, and gave himself for me."*

THE PROOF OF OUR FAITH BY THE TRIAL. *(I Peter 1:9 -Receiving the end of your faith, even the salvation of your souls.)*

- God becomes more real to us as a result of the trial.

- We draw closer to God as a result of the trial.

- We can testify of His love, help and deliverance from the trial.

- Your testimony on God's provision through your trial can bring others around you hope and cause them to draw closer to God. (*James 4:8 - Draw nigh to God, and he will draw nigh to you.*)

- The trial of our faith, proves God's love for us, proves God's provision, and it proves it to those around us as well.

IN CONCLUSION: We learned about the **Paradox** of the trial, The **Preciousness** of the trial, the **Praise** in the trial, the **Position** of security in the trial and the **Proof** of our faith in the trial. Sometimes we don't understand the trial, we might not ever understand the trial, that is the **Paradox** of the trial, but don't let that take away from the **preciousness** of God to us in the trial.

Remember to Praise God in the trial. Don't forget your **position** of security in the trial and thank God for the **Proof** of our faith as a result of the trial.

Peace in the Storm
- Part 2

> **God is What we Need!**

God is What we Need!

> **Matthew 11:28** – *"Come unto me, all ye that labour and are heavy laden, and I will give you rest."*

INTRODUCTION: Sometimes things seem impossible; impossible to do, impossible to overcome, impossible to endure or impossible to handle. But the Bible tells us all things, even the things that seem impossible to us and impossible to us, even for God to do, are possible (*Luke 18:27 – And he said, The things which are impossible with men are possible with God.*)

LIFE CAN BE EXHAUSTING - Life is often exhausting to us physically, mentally and spiritually – events in life can be too much for you to bear, too much for you to mentally accept, too much for you to

comprehend, too hurtful, too sorrowful –
but Jesus offers rest for our weary and
burdened souls (*Matthew 11:28-30 – Come
unto me, all ye that labour and are heavy
laden, and I will give you rest. Take my
yoke upon you, and learn of me; for I am
meek and lowly in heart: and ye shall find
rest unto your souls. For my yoke is easy,
and my burden is light.*) – It is often hard to
rest in the Lord, but what great peace we
have when we do.

LIFE CAN BRING FEAR - Often
you can be afraid of things in your life. You
can be afraid of the reality you find yourself
in, afraid of the circumstances you are
facing, afraid of the events that are
transpiring in your life – but God will
strengthen and help us as we face these
situations. You do not need to have the
strength or ability to go through these times
in your life. God will give you the strength
and grace that you need moment by
moment (*Isaiah 41:10 – Fear thou not; for
I am with thee: be not dismayed; for I am*

thy God: I will strengthen thee; yea, I will help thee; yea, I will uphold thee with the right hand of my righteousness.) When you are worried or anxious, God cares for you, cast your cares on Him (*I Peter 5:7 – Casting all your care upon him; for he careth for you.*)

IN CONCLUSION: Sometimes we may feel all alone, that we are going through something those around us do not understand. We may feel lonely and neglected, we may even feel distant from God; but the Lord promises to never leave us or forsake us. We may not seek Him out sometimes, and try to do something on our own; but He is with us through it in spite of us not seeking Him at those moments (*Hebrews 13:5 – … for he hath said, I will never leave thee, nor forsake thee.*)

Peace in the Storm
- Part 3

Trusting God in
the Trial

Trusting God in the Trial

Romans 8:35-39 *"Who shall separate us from the love of Christ? shall tribulation, or distress, or persecution, or famine, or nakedness, or peril, or sword? As it is written, For thy sake we are killed all the day long; we are accounted as sheep for the slaughter. Nay, in all these things we are more than conquerors through him that loved us. For I am persuaded, that neither death, nor life, nor angels, nor principalities, nor powers, nor things present, nor things to come, Nor height, nor depth, nor any other creature, shall be able to separate us from the love of God, which is in Christ Jesus our Lord."*

INTRODUCTION: David went through a lot of trials and trouble in his life. He faced the giant none other was willing to face and he killed Goliath – with God's help and guidance. What giants are you facing right now? What obstacle has presented itself in your life? Perhaps it is a financial giant, a problem relationship giant, a trial at work or school giant, a health concern giant or perhaps it is the giant of guilt or the giant of losing someone in your life that was dear and beloved to you. (*John 16:33 – These things I have spoken unto you, that in me ye might have peace. In the world ye shall have tribulation: but be of good cheer; I have overcome the world.*)

DON'T LOSE YOUR FAITH - David went on to be hunted by Saul for doing nothing wrong but willing to live his life according to God's plan and purpose.

David lived in caves in the wilderness; but David kept his faith. What trials are you going through that are no fault of your own? – give those cares and give those concerns over to God; and don't lose your faith in Him. Just like David did, though under heavy persecution and facing many trials, he kept his faith in God. Don't lose your hope or faith, with the Lord there is always hope for a better tomorrow. (***Lamentations 3:22-24*** *-It is of the LORD'S mercies that we are not consumed, because his compassions fail not. They are new every morning: great is thy faithfulness. The LORD is my portion, saith my soul; therefore will I hope in him.*)

WHY LORD? - David later went over to the Philistines; he continued to suffer many things. Many times he did not have anything to eat. – Why? Have you ever asked why? Why must I go through this trial, this tribulation, this hardship or this loss? The Bible tells us God does everything for a purpose – why didn't God make David's circumstances easier for him? Because God was training David to be a king! What could God be training you for with the circumstances you are currently facing? What could you learn from that trial? How could God use you in the future as a result of that tribulation? What could that loss you are facing lead you to in the future? We do not know the answers to these questions. We must though, however difficult it can be at the moment, we must, like David did, keep our faith in God. Trust in Him, rely on Him and continue to look for how what you are going through can be used for His honor and Glory. (*I Peter 1:6-9 – Wherein ye greatly rejoice, though now for a season, if need be, ye are in heaviness through manifold temptations: That the trial of your faith, being much more precious than of gold that perisheth, though it be tried with fire, might be found unto praise and honour and glory at the appearing of Jesus Christ: Whom having not seen, ye love; in whom, though now ye see him not, yet believing, ye rejoice with joy unspeakable and full of glory: Receiving the end of your faith, even the salvation of your souls.*)

HOW IS YOUR HEART? - In *Acts 13* verse 22 the Bible says "*he raised up unto them David to be their king; to whom also he gave testimony, and said, I have found David the son of Jesse, <u>a man after mine own heart, which shall fulfil all my will.</u>*" How is your heart lining up with God's? Are you willing to fulfill His will in your life? David in his life made many mistakes, caused many of his own problems when he strayed from God and God's will for his life. Do not allow yourself to make those same mistakes of straying from God in your time of trial, don't try to do it alone, do not allow yourself to become bitter at the situation.

IN CONCLUSION: As hard as it is to hear, as hard as it may be to think, as hard as it may be to believe – <u>but God does work everything out for</u>

the good to those who are called according to His purpose and those who confess Him as their Savior. God is our safe haven; He is our strength in time of weakness and trouble. (*Psalm 46:1* – *God is our refuge and strength, a very present help in trouble.* & *Romans 8:28* – *And we know that all things work together for good to them that love God, to them who are the called according to his purpose.*)

Peace in the Storm - Part 4

Encourage Yourself in the Lord

Encourage Yourself in the Lord

> ***I Samuel 30:6*** – *"And David was greatly distressed; for the people spake of stoning him, because the soul of all the people was grieved, every man for his sons and for his daughters: <u>but David encouraged himself in the LORD his God</u>"*.
>
> We need to turn to the Lord when we are *"greatly distressed"*, when we are *"grieved"* over a loss or a situation and remember to............................ **ENCOURAGE OURSELVES IN THE LORD!**

INTRODUCTION: *I Samuel 27:1, 5-7 – "And David said in his heart, I shall now perish one day by the hand of*

Saul: there is nothing better for me than that I should speedily escape into the land of the Philistines; and Saul shall despair of me, to seek me any more in any coast of Israel: so shall I escape out of his hand. And David said unto Achish, If I have now found grace in thine eyes, let them give me a place in some town in the country, that I may dwell there: for why should thy servant dwell in the royal city with thee? Then Achish gave him Ziklag that day: wherefore Ziklag pertaineth unto the kings of Judah unto this day. And the time that David dwelt in the country of the Philistines was a full year and four months." David fled from Israel and Saul and went into the Land of the Philistines to keep himself and his family and men safe from Saul's pursuit. Achish gave the city of Ziklag to David as a dwelling place, a place of safety and rest for his men and his family. Ziklag was where they lived when not in battles and where David's family lived.

David departs company; and his service to Achish ends. He heads back to Ziklag and to his family and a place of comfort and rest. *(I Samuel 29: 6-7, 11 - Then Achish called David, and said unto him, Surely, as the LORD liveth, thou hast been upright, and thy going out and thy coming in with me in the host is good in my sight: for I have not found evil in thee since the day of thy coming unto me unto this day: nevertheless the lords favour thee not. Wherefore now return, and go in peace, that thou displease not the lords of the Philistines. So David and his men rose up early to depart in the morning, to return into the land of the Philistines. And the Philistines went up to Jezreel.)* After David departs from Achish, he, along with his, men make the three days march from the camp of the Philistines to Ziklag. They were battle weary, travel weary and hoping to find rest in their houses and joy in their families; but a black and dismal scene presented itself.

HIS HOME HAD BEEN DISTURBED *(I Samuel 30:1-2 - And it came to pass, when David and his men were come to Ziklag on the third day, that the Amalekites had invaded the south, and Ziklag, and smitten Ziklag, and burned it with fire; And had taken the women captives, that were therein: they slew not any, either great or small, but carried them away, and went on their way.)* Have you ever come home or come to someone or someplace needing to find rest and comfort there, only to find it turned upside down and all that it once was is gone?

David and his men at this point don't know if any of their family members are even alive. They just find their homes burned up and destroyed and all their loved ones are gone. God is always working on our behalf. We might not see it, we might not realize it, but He is always working on

42

our behalf. For all David knew, his family was dead, but God had worked in the hearts of the Amalekites to carry off all the women and children and to kill none. (*I Sameul 30:2... they slew not any...*) You might be going through a hard time, but do not despair too long, the Lord is intervening in the events of life on your behalf. (*Jeremiah 1:19 - And they shall fight against thee; but they shall not prevail against thee; for I am with thee, saith the LORD, to deliver thee.*) **William Shakespeare** said this *"Now, God be praised, that to believing souls gives light in darkness, comfort in despair."*

HIS PLACE OF SAFETY HAD BEEN VIOLATED (*I Samuel 30:3 - So David and his men came to the city, and, behold, it was burned with fire; and their wives, and their sons, and their daughters, were taken captives.*) Do you have a "safe place"? A place you know you can always go to for comfort and love? A place you keep in high esteem and regard? Has that "safe place" ever been violated? Has anyone ever damaged it? Hurt you there? Let you down? The Lord can and will always be there to be a refuge for you in times like this. (*Psalm 9:9 - The LORD also will be a refuge for the oppressed, a refuge in times of trouble.*) This is what has happened to David here. He was coming home to his "safe place" after a long time in battle and a long march home, only to find someone had violated his home and his family; when we are at a point like this in life, turn to the Lord. (*Psalm 18:6 - In my distress I called upon the LORD, and cried unto my God: he heard my voice out of his temple, and my cry came before him, even into his ears.*)

HIS FAMILY HAD BEEN RIPPED APART (*I Samuel 30:4-5 - Then David and the people that were with him lifted up their voice and <u>wept, until they had no more power to weep</u>. And David's two wives were taken captives, Ahinoam the Jezreelitess, and Abigail the wife of Nabal the*

Carmelite.) <u>Have you ever wept till you had no more power to weep</u>? Have you ever cried so much there were no tears left to shed? Has the world as you know it ever crumbled down around you and fell apart and you stood helpless, powerless to do anything about it? Then give it to the Lord - don't try to bare it alone. (***Psalm 55:22*** - *Cast thy burden upon the LORD, and he shall sustain thee: he shall never suffer the righteous to be moved. &* ***Psalm 50:15*** - *And call upon me in the day of trouble: I will deliver thee, and thou shalt glorify me.)* The Lord is our hope. Don't lose hope in your life. If you have the Lord you always have hope.

David speaks of times like these in his Psalms. If you are going through a rough time turn to the Lord, run to Him. Give it to Him. Cling to Him and don't let go. If the whole world seems like it is spinning out of control, if your Heart is overwhelmed, cling to the Rock of your salvation.

- ***Psalm 61:2*** – *"From the end of the earth will I cry unto thee, <u>when my heart is overwhelmed: lead me to the rock that is higher than I</u>."*

- ***Psalm 62:8*** – *"Trust in him at all times; ye people, <u>pour out your heart before him</u>: God is a refuge for us."*

- ***Psalm 62:2*** – *"He only is my rock and my salvation; <u>he is my defence</u>; I shall not be greatly moved."*

- ***Psalm 63:3*** – *"Because thy lovingkindness is better than life, my lips shall praise thee."*

- ***Psalm 63:7*** – *"Because thou hast been my help, therefore in the shadow of thy wings will I rejoice."*

Keep in mind when you are going through a storm in life, of who controls the storms in our life. *(Psalm 148:8 - Fire, and hail; snow, and vapours; stormy wind fulfilling his word: & Mark 34:39-40 - And he arose, and rebuked the wind, and said unto the sea, Peace, be still. And the wind ceased, and there was a great calm. And he said unto them, Why are ye so fearful? how is it that ye have no faith?)* Have faith in the Master of the storm to see you through the storm. He will see you through to the other side. He has the power to calm the storm in your life. *"Peace, be still"* is what he said and peace is what happened. If you need peace in your life turn to the Lord Jesus who with but a spoken word can bring the peace you need. **Henry Wadsworth Longfellow** speaking of how big problems can appear had this thought *"The nearer the dawn the darker the night"* – The problem may appear the biggest when the solution is the closest.

HIS FRIENDS TURNED ON HIM

(I Samuel 30:6b - for the people spake of stoning him, because the soul of all the people was grieved, every man for his sons and for his daughters:) Have you ever had friends turn on you? Have you ever been going through a problem and have your friends let you down. Have you ever been unjustly blamed for a problem? David has been there too. In this verse we see that some of his "mighty men" start to turn on him and blame him for the terrible situation they are all in. Well, be encouraged in the Lord Jesus because we have a friend that sticketh closer than a brother. Like the song says *"What a friend we have in Jesus"*. And we do- we have the best friend in the world! He will always be there for us to talk to day or night. He will always help us. He will always love us and He will never turn on us. *(**Proverbs 18:24b** - and there is a friend that sticketh closer than a brother.& **Hebrews 13:5c** - for he hath said, I will never leave thee, nor forsake thee.)*

David's faith is being greatly tested here. If we are to ever have a strong faith, expect some tests to come. Just because we go through some tough times does not mean the Lord has turned on us or forsaken us. Great faith will be tested. *(James 1:3 - Knowing this, that the trying of your faith worketh patience.) - "I would go the deeps a hundred times to cheer a downcast spirit. It is good for me to have been afflicted, that I might know how to speak a word in season to one that is weary."* **Charles H. Spurgeon.** – Use your experiences in trials and getting through them to help others when they are going through a problem.

HE WAS GREALTY DISTRESSED (*I Samuel 30:6a- And David was greatly distressed;)* David was going through an incredibly hard trial here. He was as distressed as a man can ever get at this moment. Part of the reason for this great distress is he had not yet given it over to the Lord.

- He found out about the terrible situation

- He wept over it till he could weep no more.

- The blame game had started.

- He became "*greatly distressed*" – but had not yet turned it over to the only One that could help him.

If you are going through a problem like this turn to the Lord immediately; don't delay, don't try to solve it on your own, just turn it over to the Lord. *(**John 14:1** - Let not your heart be troubled: ye believe in God, believe also in me.)* Don't let your hearts be troubled over your problems, give them to the Lord. Don't delay! Cast all your cares on the Lord. *(**I Peter 5:7** - Casting all your care upon him; for he careth for you.)*

HE ENCOURAGED HIMSELF IN THE LORD *(**I Samuel 30:6c** - but David* *encouraged himself in the LORD his God.)* David encouraged his heart in the Lord. He did the only thing he could do. *(Isaiah 41:10 -Fear thou not; for I am with thee: be not dismayed; for I am thy God: I will strengthen thee; yea, I will help thee; yea, I will uphold thee with the right hand of my righteousness.)* When all is crumbling down around you, when you have nowhere else to turn, when your burden overwhelms you, you can turn to the Lord. He will sustain you. He will encourage you. *(Isaiah 40:31 - But they that wait upon the LORD shall renew their strength; they shall mount up with wings as eagles; they shall run, and not be weary; and they shall walk, and not faint.)*

IN CONCLUSION: Sometimes all we have is the Lord. Sometimes all we can do is to encourage ourselves in the Lord. *(Psalm 142:5a - I cried unto thee, O LORD: I said, Thou art my refuge ... & Psalm 31:24 -Be of good courage,* *and he shall strengthen your heart, all ye that hope in the LORD.)* We need to remember to encourage ourselves in the Lord. It doesn't just happen; we have to seek Him out. Get in His word, pray, go to church, seek council. *(Psalm 122:1 - I was glad when they said unto me, Let us go into the house of the LORD.)* Read His word. Let Him talk to you through His word. Pray about it. Be in a constant state of prayer about it. *(James 5:16c - The effectual fervent prayer of a righteous man availeth much.)*

Peace in the Storm - Part 5

Inquire at the Lord for Direction

Inquire at the Lord for Direction

> ***I Samuel 30:8*** *– "And <u>David</u> <u>inquired at the LORD,</u> saying, Shall I pursue after this troop? shall I overtake them? And he answered him, Pursue: for thou shalt surely overtake them, and without fail recover all."*
>
> We need to do what David did here. When faced with adversity he first *"encouraged himself in the Lord"* and then to get direction as to what to do he *"enquired at the Lord."*

INTRODUCTION: David had just left his service to Achish. He was battle weary. He and his men travelled a three days march back home to get some rest and renewal with their families. David and his men came to the town they were staying at, Ziklag, only to find it in ruins. It had been burned down and all their possessions carried off. Their families were missing. David and his mighty men it says in **verse 4** *"lifted up their voice and wept, until they had no more power to weep."* At this low point David turns to the Lord; it says in **verse 6** that *"David encouraged himself in the LORD"*. Now David turns to the Lord and seeks Him out for wisdom and direction as to what He should do.

THE PROVIDENTIAL DEPEND- ENCE OF DAVID - After David *"encouraged himself in the Lord"*, he immediately sought ought the Lords council and direction. (*I Samuel 30:7* - *And David said to Abiathar the priest, Ahimelech's son, I pray thee, bring me hither the ephod. And Abiathar brought thither the ephod to David.*)

Ephod – was a religious object that was used to get close to the Lord and get direction and guidance from Him. Like we would turn to our Bible or prayer today to get close to the Lord and get guidance from Him.

David depended on guidance, grace and strength from the Lord in his time of distress. Some people can get bitter and impatient in a time of distress but David in his time of distress turned to the Lord the one who could help him. *(Mathew 11:28 - Come unto me, all ye that labour and are heavy laden, and I will give you rest.)* **Matthew Henry** put it this way "*When David was at his wits' end he was not at his faith's end.*" We need to submissively place our dependence for all our needs in the hands of our Heavenly Father. *(Mark 14:36 - And he said, Abba, Father, all things are possible unto thee; take away this cup from me: nevertheless not what I will, but what thou wilt.)*

PRAY FOR GUIDANCE: I'm sure David already had the thought to go after the people that did this great injustice to him and his mighty men. No one would have thought badly of him for doing so. But David prayed to the Lord for guidance first. He sought the Lord out first. He did not jump the gun. *(I Samuel 30:8a - And David inquired at the LORD, saying, Shall I pursue after this troop? shall I overtake them?)* David did not rely on his own wisdom but prayed to the Lord for an answer as to what to do. (*I Corinthians 2:5 -That your faith should not stand in the wisdom of men, but in the power of God.)*

David in seeking the Lord out first acknowledges his submission and dependence on the Lord. – Are you submitting yourself to the Lord? The Lord answers David's prayer. *(I Samuel 30:8b - And he answered him, Pursue: for thou shalt surely overtake them, and without fail recover all.)* **President George Washington** said this about seeking and doing the Lord's will; *"Make sure you are doing what God wants you to do – then do it with all your might!"*

PURSUE! – THE ANSWER DAVID SUBMISSIVELY PRAYED FOR – Sometimes when we think we know what God's answer to our prayer will be, we still need to get on our knees and submissively depend on Him for the answer before we act. *(I Samuel 30:9a - So David went, he and the six hundred men that were with him, and came to the brook Besor)* David prayed to the Lord for help in his time of distress. The Lord gave him a clear answer to his prayer. *"So David went"*; the Lord spoke and immediately David followed the Lords direction. (*Luke 5:24-25a - But that ye may know that the Son of man hath power upon earth to forgive sins, (he said unto the sick of the palsy,) I say unto thee, Arise, and take up thy couch, and go into thine house. And <u>immediately</u> he rose up before them...)*

When the Lord "speaks" to us we need to be willing to immediately do what he leads us to do. Don't hesitate once you get the answer from the Lord pursue it to completion. Trust the Lords direction and answers to prayer and be willing to obey His answer, whatever that answer may be, or wherever obeying that answer may take you.

Pursue! – The path the Lord has put you on even if it looks like it is not going to work out. Do not rely on your own assessment of the situation. When it lcoks like everything is falling apart PURSUE if the Lord has told you to. *(I Samuel 30:9b-10 -and came to the brook Besor, where those that were left behind stayed. But David pursued, he and four hundred men: for two hundred abode behind, which were so faint that they could not go over the brook Besor.)* "*But David pursued*" – Some adversity came right away. He followed the Lords answer to prayer, but 1/3 of his men were too physically and emotionally weary to continue.

David loses 1/3 of his men. Now he has to go after those that burned down Ziklag and abducted his family with just 400 men. *"But David pursued"* – Don't lose faith in the face of adversity. If you know it is the Lords will, don't waver, don't stop, PURSUE! *(Proverbs 24:10 - If thou faint in the day of adversity, thy strength is small.)* Sometimes the Lord will reveal His will to us, then test us to see how determined we are to follow his will. *(James 1:12 - Blessed is the man that endureth temptation: for when he is tried, he shall receive the crown of life, which the Lord hath promised to them that love him.)* – *"temptation"* in this verse means trial.

PROVIDE FOR OTHERS NEEDS IN THE MIDST OF YOUR TRIAL: Don't walk around with tunnel vision when you are trying to do the Lords will. Be willing to be detoured off your planned route for the day. That very detour may be planned for you by God to help answer a need you have. *(I Samuel 30:11-12 - And they found an Egyptian in the field, and brought him to David, and gave him bread, and he did eat; and they made him drink water; And they gave him a piece of a cake of figs, and two clusters of raisins: and when he had eaten, his spirit came again to him: for he had eaten no bread, nor drunk any water, three days and three nights.)* Don't always just think of yourself when you are going through a trial. Seek to be used of God to meet others needs too.

David and his men gave out of their own necessity to meet the needs of this Egyptian boy. Be willing to be used of God to meet others needs both physically and spiritually. (*Mark 12:44 - For all they did cast in of their abundance; but she of her want did cast in all that she had, even all her living.)* David and his men in their time of great distress and heartbreak saw a need that someone else had and took of their own provision and time to meet that need. Ministering to others in their time of need can be the best therapy for helping us through our own time of distress and need. *(Galatians 6:2 - Bear ye one another's burdens, and so fulfil the law of Christ.*

PRUDENCE OF THE PROVISION: God revealed more of His will and answer to David's prayer as he was willing to stop and help meet someone else's needs. *(I Samuel 30:13 -14 - And David said unto him, To whom belongest thou? and whence art thou? And he said, I am a young man of Egypt, servant to an Amalekite; and my master left me, because three days ago I fell sick. We made an invasion upon the south of the Cherethites, and upon the coast which belongeth to Judah, and upon the south of Caleb; and we burned Ziklag with fire.)* Though David and his men were in a hurry, they stopped and helped this Egyptian. And it turned out to be a Divine appointment. Because helping this young man was the key to finding their loved ones. (*I John 4:21 - And this commandment have we from him, That he who loveth God love his brother also.*) The Egyptian gave an account of his party and what they had been doing. And his party was the very party David and his men were looking for.

The Lord will do things like this. We get ourselves in a hurry going about doing a lot of works for Him, but what He would really like us to do is stop, slow down, and minister to someone's needs. The Lord will bless your efforts for Him. In your time of distress take time to help others. The help you give others may lead to the answers you were praying for. (*I John 3:11 - For this is the message that ye heard from the beginning, that we should love one another.*)

THE PLEASING PLEASURE IN FOLLOWING THE LORDS WILL IN SPITE OF ADVERSITY: David sought to get closer to God is his time of distress. He prayed for the Lords will and he kept on doing the Lords will even though he encountered setbacks along the way. *(I Samuel 30:19 - And there was nothing lacking to them, neither small nor great, neither sons nor daughters, neither spoil, nor any thing that they had taken to them: <u>David recovered all</u>.)* The Egyptian boy led them to the camp of the Amalekites (those who burned Ziklag and kidnapped their families). David and his mighty men then attacked the Amelikites and destroyed them. *(I Samuel 30:17 - And David smote them from the twilight even unto the evening of the next day: and there escaped not a man of them, save four hundred young men, which rode upon camels, and fled.)*

David surprised them with the attack. The spoil the Amalekites had taken was recovered. All their families were reunited and much more was gained in the process. *(Hebrews 11:6 - But without faith it is impossible to please him: for he that cometh to God must believe that he is, and* *that he is a <u>rewarder of them that diligently seek him</u>.)* God promises to reward those that seek diligently to do His will. They took all that belonged to the Amelikites besides what they originally had. God loves to bless us with even more than we prayed for. *(**Ephesians 3:20**- Now unto him that is able to do exceeding abundantly above all that we ask or think, according to the power that worketh in us,)* Sometimes if God was to give us only what we prayed for, we would miss out on a blessing. Don't limit God with your prayers of little faith. Claim the promises of God and boldly pray to your Heavenly Father. *(**Hebrews 4:16** - Let us therefore come boldly unto the throne of grace, that we may obtain mercy, and find grace to help in time of need.)*

Now those men who in verse 6 spoke of stoning David were now praising his name. God can restore your reputation if it has been unjustly sullied by someone. *(**Psalm 60:12** - Through God we shall do* *valiantly: for he it is that shall tread down our enemies.)*

IN CONCLUSION: God rewards the faithfulness of his people. *(Proverbs 28:20a - A faithful man shall abound with blessings:)* God will take care of his people. *(John 14:27 - Peace I leave with you, my peace I give unto you: not as the world giveth, give I unto you. Let not your heart be troubled, neither let it be afraid.)* God can help you through your problem to the other side of it. God can help you recover all like He did with David and bless you with more beside. *(Luke 18:27 - And he said, The things which are impossible with men are possible with God.)*

Peace in the Storm
- Part 6

> ## "God is our Refuge and Strength"

"God is our Refuge and Strength"

> **Psalm 46:1** - *"God is our refuge and strength, a very present help in trouble."*

INTRODUCTION: I had the thoughts of this section on my mind for a long time but never felt peace about sharing them or writing them down. My Pastor preached a message one Sunday evening and he referenced a verse that was very precious to me in a very rough period in my life. After his message the Lord started directing my thoughts to this passage, and this message and to write them down and share them. *Psalm 46:1* was my life verse for many years. It is still very precious to me. Without this verse I probably would not be the person I am today. This message and the thoughts of this message are very much of a personal nature to me.

PROBLEMS IN LIFE - Have you ever been in a rough patch in your life? Has it ever felt like your world was collapsing around you? Have all your hopes and dreams ever been shattered before? Well if you have or are presently experiencing anything like this, you should thank God for this verse and the truths held in it. We find in this verse:

- Hope in God

- The presence of God

- A promise of God

- The Power of God

- And because of that power we can have a path to restoration through God!

CAUSES OF PROBLEMS IN OUR LIFE

- Our own failures or bad decisions

- Others failures or bad decisions-innocent victim

- Or circumstances brought about having to do with health, finance, a loss or other things

- Either way, our hope and path to restoration and healing lies in God and His Word!

WE CAN THINK OF SOME COLOSSAL FAILURES IN THE BIBLE

- **Abraham** – lied twice about his wife Sarah.

- **David** – committed adultery and orchestrated murder to cover it up.

- **Peter** – denied Christ.

- **Paul** – consented to the murder & persecutions of Christians.

All of these men had something in common. They all had a second chance. They served the God of the second chance. I am personally thankful I serve the same God they served – <u>The God of the second chance!</u>

The following is a poem I wrote about **Psalm 46:1** while going through a particularly rough time in my life.

<u>Remember This</u>
*(*Written in Powell, TN – March 18th 1997*)*

God is our refuge, remember this,
God is our refuge, when things are amiss,
God is our refuge when things are going well,
God is our refuge, remember this well,

God is our strength, remember this,
God is our strength, remember His nearness,

God is our strength when we are week,
God is our strength, strength for the meek,

God is our help, remember this,
God is our help, a very present help – with
no absence,
God is our help, a help in time of trouble,
God is our help, with His help all things to
do we are able.

PERPETUAL HOPE WITH GOD –
(***Psalm 46:2a*** - *"Therefore will not we*
fear") Why can we live without fear? –
Because we have hope with God.
(***Lamentations 3:21-26*** - *This I recall to my*
mind, therefore have I hope. It is of the
LORD'S mercies that we are not consumed,
because his compassions fail not. They are
new every morning: great is thy
faithfulness. The LORD is my portion, saith
my soul; therefore will I hope in him. The
LORD is good unto them that wait for him,
to the soul that seeketh him. It is good that
a man should both hope and quietly wait
for the salvation of the LORD.) You may

think all hope is lost – but it is not. If you are a Christian you are never without hope! *(I Timothy 1:1 – "Paul, an apostle of Jesus Christ by the commandment of God our Saviour, and Lord Jesus Christ, which is our hope;")* So who is our hope? How do we have hope? The Lord Jesus is the source of our hope. If you are a Christian you always have hope.

PRESENCE OF GOD – *(Psalm 46:1 – God is our refuge and strength, a <u>very present</u> help in trouble.)* God is not just a present help in time of trouble, He is a VERY PRESENT HELP in time of trouble. Right when you need the Lord the most, He is there the most for you – you just need to seek Him out. You need to turn to Him and ask Him for the help you need. Run to the Lord Jesus when you are having problems or struggles He will always be there for you. God will give you comfort when you need it most. *(Psalm 71:21 – "Thou shalt increase my greatness, and comfort me on every side.")*

PROMISE OF GOD (*Psalm 46:1a - God is our refuge*) – He promises to see us through the storms of our life. He promises to be the "*refuge*" we need. *Mark 4:35-39* says "*And the same day, when the even was come, <u>he saith unto them, Let us pass over unto the other side</u>. And when they had sent away the multitude, they took him even as he was in the ship. And there were also with him other little ships. And there arose a great storm of wind, and the waves beat into the ship, so that it was now full. And he was in the hinder part of the ship, asleep on a pillow: and they awake him, and say unto him, Master, carest thou not that we perish? And he arose, and rebuked the wind, and said unto the sea, Peace, be still. And the wind ceased, and there was a great calm.*" and chapter *Mark 5:1* says "*<u>And they came over unto the other side</u> of the sea, into the country of the Gadarenes.*" – Notice in the first passage we read, Jesus said "*Let us pass over to the other side*" and in verse 1 of chapter 5 of *Mark* the Bible says *"And they came over unto the other side"*

Notice Jesus did not promise a problem free journey to the other side, but He was there with them in the storm. (**Psalm 46:1** - *a very present help in trouble."*) And all they had to do to get the storm in their life to calm down was to turn to Jesus and give the problem over to Him. God promises to be *"our refuge"* in the storms of life. He does not promise a problem free life – but He does promise to be there for us and help us through those storms of our life.

Also, let's look at one more promise of God. **I John 1:9** says *"If we confess our sins, he is faithful and just to forgive us our sins, and to cleanse us from all unrighteousness."* If the storms in our life are self caused – God promises to forgive our sins that caused that storm too.

Storms of Life
(Written in Powell, TN – March 16th 1997)

When you see troubles coming on the
horizon,
When you hear the thunder and see the
lightening,
When the wind howls, the rain falls and the
storm is raging,
When the storms of life are at their worst,
don't fear!
Remember down in the back of your ship
the Lord is near,
Trust the Lord for what He has promised,
And remember what the Lord has said,
"Let us pass over unto the other side."
Call on the Lord and He will be by your
side,
To command the winds and the rain to
subside,
Remember with three words the storm He
did quell,
"Peace be still", "Peace be still" and all
was well.

POWER OF GOD – (***Psalm 46:1*** – *God is*
our refuge and strength) – GOD IS THE
SOURCE OF OUR STRENTH. God uses

circumstances in our life to lead us to humility and dependence on Him. This foundation of humility and dependence He can then build upon – He can rebuild your life anew on this foundation that is anchored in Him. He will give you the strength to rebuild your life. *(Job 12:13 - With him is wisdom and strength, he hath counsel and understanding.)* He will give you strength to renew your joy. *(Psalm 27:1 - The LORD is my light and my salvation; whom shall I fear? the LORD is the strength of my life; of whom shall I be afraid?)*

PATH TO RESTORATION – OUR GOD IS THE GOD OF THE SECOND CHANCE *(Jonah 3:1 – "And the word of the LORD came unto Jonah the second time").* Aren't you thankful for the "second time" God came to you? Aren't you Thankful for the second chance the Lord gave you? Remember the heroes of the Bible I mentioned earlier – Abraham, David, Peter and Paul – where would they be, but for the second chance the Lord gave them?

God gives us a path to restoration for all us in *Ephesians 4:31* – *"Let all bitterness, and wrath, and anger, and clamour, and evil speaking, be put away from you, with all malice: And be ye kind one to another, tenderhearted, forgiving one another, even as God for Christ's sake hath forgiven you."* These verses give us some instruction of how to be to others who are starting over, who are in the beginning part of their second chance. Don't be bitter or angry to them. Don't speak evil things about them or gossip about them. Instead be kind to them and tenderhearted to them. Be forgiving to them.

IN CONCLUSION: Remember our God is the God of the second chance. If you are going through a rough time in your life turn to Him. He is a very present help in your time of trouble. Don't lose hope in your distress; the Lord will see you through to the other side of the storm in your life. He will be with you, if you are a Christian, all through the storm. Turn to Him for help He will be your *"refuge"* in the storm of your life.

After it All
(Written in Clinton, TN – November 6th 1997)

After the valleys, you have the mountain tops,
After the trials, the blessings don't stop,
After the pain, comes hope for tomorrow,
After the tears, He lifts up our sorrow,
After the storm, the sun shines brighter,
After the heartbreak, the joy is greater,
After your sadness, comes greater gladness,
After your prayers, your burden is less,
After it all, His love is pure,
After it all, your happiness is secure!

REFERENCES

Henry, Matthew. *Matthew Henry's Commentary* Grand Rapids, MI: Zondervan 1961

Graham, Billy. *The Billy Graham Christian Worker's Handbook* World Wide Publications Minneapolis, MN 1996

Atkinson, David M. *The Heart of a Shepherd* Grace and Glory Publishing Dyer, IN 2001

Recker, Matthew. *Living on the Edge of Eternity* BJU Press 2007